TROUBLED WORLD

AFRICA: POSTCOLONIAL CONFLICT

DAVID DOWNING

Heinemann
LIBRARY

www.heinemann.co.uk
Visit our website to find out more information about **Heinemann Library** books.

To order:
☎ Phone 44 (0) 1865 888066
🖹 Send a fax to 44 (0) 1865 314091
🖳 Visit the Heinemann Bookshop at www.heinemann.co.uk to browse our catalogue and order online.

First published in Great Britain by Heinemann Library, Halley Court, Jordan Hill, Oxford OX2 8EJ, part of Harcourt Education.
Heinemann is a registered trademark of Harcourt Education Ltd.

© Harcourt Education Ltd 2003
The moral right of the proprietor has been asserted.

Editorial: Geoff Barker, Nancy Dickmann, Louise Galpine, Kate Taylor
Design: Ron Kamen, Rob Norridge
Picture Research: Rachel Tisdale
Cartographer: Stefan Chabluk
Production: Séverine Ribierre

Originated by Dot Gradations
Printed and bound in China by South China Printing Company

ISBN 0 431 183643
07 06 05 04 03
10 9 8 7 6 5 4 3 2 1

British Library Cataloguing in Publication Data
Downing, David, 1946–
Africa: postcolonial conflict. – (Troubled World)
960
A full catalogue record for this book is available from the British Library.

Acknowledgements
The publishers would like to thank the following for permission to reproduce photographs: Corbis p.55; Corbis pp.57 (Adrian Arbib), 37 (Baci), 50 (Howard Davies), 9 (Owen Franken), 53 (Bill Gentile), 15 (Daniel Laine), 18 (Neal Preston),19 (Chris Rainier), 31 (David Turnley); Popperfoto pp. 6, 16, 24, 26, 27, 28, 32, 54; Popperfoto pp. 38 (Alexander Joe), 10, 14, 21, 35, 39, 40, 42, 43, 45, 46, 48, 49 (Reuters), 30 (UPI); Still pictures p.59 (Ron Giling); Topham/AP p.23.

Cover photograph of Zairean refugees heading towards Rwandan border, November 1996. Reproduced with permission of Topham/AP.

Every effort has been made to contact copyright holders of any material reproduced in this book. Any omissions will be rectified in subsequent printings if notice is given to the publishers.

All the internet addresses (URLs) given in this book were valid at the time of going to press. However, due to the dynamic nature of the Internet, some addresses may have changed, or sites may have changed or ceased to exist since publication. While the author and publishers regret any inconvenience this may cause readers, no responsibility for any such changes can be accepted by either the author or the publishers.

Contents

Words that appear in the text in bold, **like this**, are explained in the glossary.

Troubled continent

Africa is the world's second largest continent, slightly more than three times the size of the USA, and 125 times the size of the UK. Much of Africa lies within the tropics, but there is considerable geographical diversity: the dense rainforests of the Congo, the fertile hills of the Great Rift Valley, the dry grasslands of the savannah and the arid deserts of the Sahara and Kalahari.

At the beginning of 2003 Africans numbered 900 million. In the last 40 years the population of Africa has increased by 300 per cent, as compared with a population increase of 60 per cent in the USA over the same period. By 2025 the continent is predicted to be home to a fifth of the world's people. Africa's people are as varied as its geography. Over 1000 languages are spoken by an even larger number of social groupings – variously called **tribes**, **clans** or **ethnic** groups. Over the last half century these groupings have been divided up, often untidily, between 53 modern states or countries.

The states which lie to the north of the Sahara Desert, mostly **Muslim** and populated by Arabic-speaking peoples, have much closer ties to the Middle East than the rest of Africa. This book is concerned with the troubled history of the states that lie between the Sahara Desert and South Africa, those states which form the bulk of black Africa. South Africa's highly distinctive recent history has earned it a book of its own in this series.

History

Until around 1000 years ago this area of Africa was a land of many different tribes with a few larger kingdoms, and it had little contact with the rest of the world. Over the next 900 years, it was slowly penetrated by other, more outgoing cultures: principally the **Arabs** of the Middle East and the sea-faring nations of north-west Europe. These intruders brought their religions – **Islam** in the north and east, **Christianity** in much of the rest – and the slave trade. A few settled, but most were content to take the continent's riches home with them. At the end of the 19th century most of Africa was formally divided into European colonies, under the direct rule of the European **colonial** powers.

This colonial period ended, with a few exceptions, in the late 1950s and early 1960s. The European administrators went home, and most of the newly independent countries set out to develop their economies along **free enterprise** lines and establish systems of government. There have been some successes. A few economies have flourished, at least for a while, and there are signs that **democracy** has taken root in some countries. But mostly there have been failures. Over the last 40 years many African countries have succumbed to brutal dictators and economic progress has been either minimal or non-existent. As poverty and hopelessness have spread, so violence has erupted both within and between states and many millions of ordinary Africans have had their already difficult lives blighted by fear and tragedy.

Why has this happened? How has Africa south of the Sahara become a continent in crisis? We must begin with the first real turning point of modern African history, independence from colonial rule.

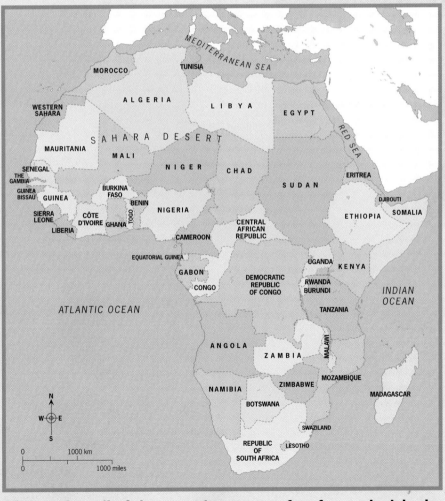

Africa today. All of the countries are now free from colonial rule.

Turning point: Independence

Europeans first came to **sub-Saharan** Africa in the 15th century, but for the next 400 years they confined themselves to building settlements on the coasts and stealing or trading everything from gold to human beings. It was not until the late 19th century, with the slave trade abolished and most of the continent explored, mapped and divided, that the European powers actually began to govern Africa on a day-to-day basis. The period of **colonial** rule lasted, in most cases, considerably less than a century. A country like Zambia, for example, was first subjected to white colonial rule in 1889 and received its independence 75 years later, in 1964.

Kenyans celebrate their independence from British rule in December 1963.

The African struggle against colonial rule gathered momentum after World War II, inspired by Japanese military successes against the white powers during the war, and successful independence struggles in India, Indonesia and Indochina. By the mid-1950s colonial rule in Africa had few supporters, and the European powers were preparing their departure. In the decade that followed Ghana's independence in 1957, the British, French and Belgians withdrew from almost all their African possessions. Only the Portuguese (in Angola, Mozambique and Portuguese Guinea) and the **white minority governments** of Southern Africa clung on to colonial power.

Real independence?

'*...nothing but a fancy-dress parade and blare of trumpets. There's nothing save a minimum of readaption, a few reforms at the top, a flag waving: and down there at the bottom an undivided mass, still living in the Middle Ages, endlessly marking time.*'
Franz Fanon's view of African independence, from his book The Wretched of the Earth, *written in the late 1950s. Fanon was a psychoanalyst and philosopher who wrote about racism and colonial rule. He was concerned that independence alone would not improve the situation of ordinary Africans, especially if the colonial powers did not help them adjust to their new status.*

The dream

Despite the obvious difficulties which lay ahead, there was, in these early years, a real sense of setting out on a great journey, a sense that Africa could overcome its difficulties and take an equal place in the family of nations. The transition to independence was, with only a few exceptions, relatively peaceful. The new states generally got on with each other. The new **Organization of African Unity (OAU)**, which came into being in 1963, played a useful role in sorting out those disputes which did arise. It also symbolized Africans' determination to take control of their own continent and its destiny.

On the economic front, following the advice of the former colonial powers, most African states adopted the same basic plan for development. The main idea was to increase sales to the developed countries of whichever product they specialized in – for example, cocoa in Ghana, coffee in Kenya – and to borrow from the developed countries against the eventual profits which they expected to make. The money borrowed would be used to diversify the economy (by creating new businesses, both industrial and agricultural) and to improve education, health care, housing and economic communications (such as roads, railways and electricity). As the new businesses took off, the African country would have more to sell abroad and less need to import goods from other countries. They would become more truly independent, and their people would become more prosperous, acquiring higher levels of health, education and material wealth. That, at least, was the hope and the dream.

There were also good reasons for doubt. These can be divided into political and economic reasons, though in practice the two were often hard to disentangle.

Difficulties – the political inheritance
The politicians who took over the leadership of the newly independent countries were, like politicians everywhere, a mixed bunch. Most had been educated in the West, and many had served in colonial administrations. Their education and lifestyle already marked them apart from the great majority of their own people.

In most cases, those involved in the struggle for independence had organized themselves into single political parties, and it was these parties which now formed the governments of the new countries. Since there had been no real domestic opposition to independence, there were few opposition parties. The new countries began life without one of the essential ingredients of **democracy** – a real choice between different contenders for government. This stored up problems for the future. One-party states tend to become **dictatorships**, and dictatorships tend to be **corrupt** and inefficient.

In most African countries the situation was further complicated by **ethnic** issues. At the time of independence Africa was still a continent of **tribes** – what we would now call ethnic groups – rather than nations. When the Europeans had divided up Africa, they had taken little notice of the existing boundaries between tribes, so most of the 'nations' created by the Europeans contained more than one ethnic group. During colonial times the Europeans had often deepened existing hostilities by favouring some groups over others. Those who formed the governments of the newly independent states, and who claimed to speak for the whole nation, often came from a single ethnic group. This inevitably created resentment among other groups, and when things went badly, they would often blame each other for the failures, and violent conflict would result.

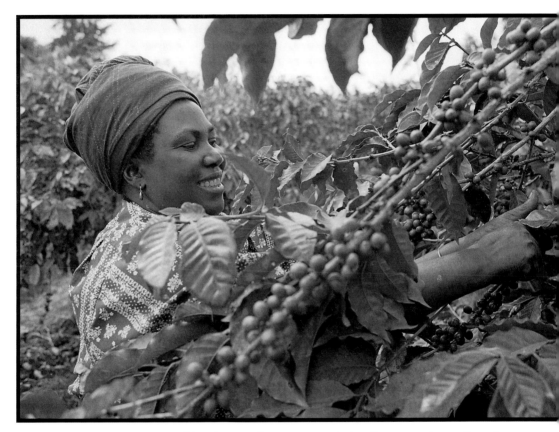

A woman picking coffee beans in Kenya, 1973. The growing of such crops was an important part of plans for development.

Africa's domestic troubles were often made worse by foreign interference. After independence, the **Cold War** between countries following a **free enterprise** system (led by the USA) and those following **communism** (led by the Soviet Union), spread to include Africa. This had one apparently useful consequence: the new African states were sometimes able to play the two **superpowers** off against each other, and to use the promise of friendship to win economic aid from one or the other. But overall, the Cold War was a disaster for Africa. If one superpower supported a particular African government, then the other

9

Biography – Julius Nyerere

Julius Nyerere (1922–99) became the first prime minister of independent Tanganyika in 1961, and the first president of Tanzania (following the union of Tanganyika and the island state of Zanzibar) in 1964. He was a strong supporter of African culture, and Tanzania became the only country in Africa to have a native tongue – Swahili – as its official language. In politics and economics he championed a form of rural **socialism** called *ujamaa* (literally 'familyhood'). It stressed the importance of self-reliance (the ability to make your own decision) and Tanzanian independence from the Western economic system. This was largely an economic failure, though it did provide notable improvements in education and health care.

Nyerere did not use power to strut the world stage or enrich himself, and in 1985 he stepped down of his own accord. Though not a saint, he was a man of principle, and was much respected throughout the continent.

Julius Nyerere, first president of Tanganyika and Tanzania, and one of Africa's most respected statesmen.

would seek to undermine that government by supporting its opponents, who often included both neighbouring states and other ethnic groups inside the country. This encouragement of national and ethnic hatreds was rendered even more deadly by a growing flood of Western- and Soviet-manufactured weaponry.

A change of identity: some African states and their new names after independence
Bechuanaland → Botswana
Zaire → Democratic Republic of the Congo
Dahomey → Benin
Northern Rhodesia → Zambia
Nyasaland → Malawi
Southern Rhodesia → Zimbabwe
South-West Africa → Namibia
Tanganyika + Zanzibar → Tanzania

Difficulties – The economic inheritance

The economic situation was no more promising than the political situation. The colonial powers failed to build educational or other training facilities that would provide a trained leadership. The new leaderships had even less experience of economic management than political administration, and most of their people lacked even basic skills such as **literacy**. When independence was given to the four states of French Equatorial Africa (Chad, the Central African Republic, Congo-Brazzaville and Gabon), there were only five university graduates between them. Improving education and creating the sort of health services that a modern work-force required would take money, but where was it to come from?

The economies of the newly independent countries were anything but independent. The old systems of **colonial preference** – which forced the colonies to sell their products to the **colonial** power at prices that suited the latter – had disappeared, but the new system of global free enterprise was not much of an improvement. Sub-Saharan Africa's main money-earners were minerals (such as copper, gold and diamonds) and crops grown specifically for the Western market (like coffee and cocoa). The prices paid for these goods, however, were set by the huge Western corporations who controlled distribution and sales, and who could pick and choose where to buy the goods. From the very beginning, the new governments of Africa had almost no control over their own economic destinies.

The Muslim/non-Muslim divide

Before colonization most Africans followed local, traditional religions. The traders and missionaries brought Islam and Christianity over with them and many Africans converted (sometimes by force). When the Europeans drew Africa's borders in the late 19th century they ignored the invisible line dividing the overwhelmingly **Muslim** north of the continent from the non-Muslim south. This line, which snakes across the continent, is not clear-cut, but the states that lie mostly to the south of it, like Ghana or Benin, have a Muslim population of 20 per cent or less, while those to the north, like Niger or Mali, have between 80 and 90 per cent. To date, there have been no significant Muslim/non-Muslim disputes in these countries. The lasting problems have come in those states that the line cuts roughly in half: for example Sudan, Nigeria and, to a lesser extent, Chad.

Sudan

The British ruled Sudan, Africa's largest country, from the end of the 19th century to 1956, but they did not rule it as one country. One administration in Khartoum looked after the **Arab** Muslims of the north (70 per cent of the population), while another in Juba looked after the black, mostly Christian, south (30 per cent). It was only in the last few years of **colonial** rule that any attempt was made to create a united administration, and almost 50 years after independence it now seems unfortunate that the attempt was made at all. Whatever the European borders suggested, and the new Muslim Arab government in Khartoum claimed, Sudan was essentially two countries disguised as one.

The new government made little attempt to improve matters, and the military rulers who took over in 1958 only made things worse. The use of the Arabic language was increasingly demanded, Friday rather than Sunday was chosen as the sabbath holiday throughout the country and Christian missionaries and southern politicians expelled. In 1963 armed resistance began in the south, led by a group which called itself Anya Nya or 'Snake Venom'. Over the next nine years around 400,000 Sudanese lost their lives as a direct result of **civil war**.

In 1972 President Nimeiry made a bold attempt at solving the problem. He told the southern provinces that they would be allowed to rule themselves, that only foreign affairs and defence would be reserved for the central government in Khartoum. But Nimeiry never put his plan into practice, and as the economy declined he became both more **dictatorial** and more aggressively Muslim. In 1983 he tried to impose Muslim **Sharia law** on the whole country. That same year the civil war re-started, this time between the government's army and the south's newly-formed Sudan People's Liberation Army. Nineteen years would pass before the next meaningful **ceasefire**.

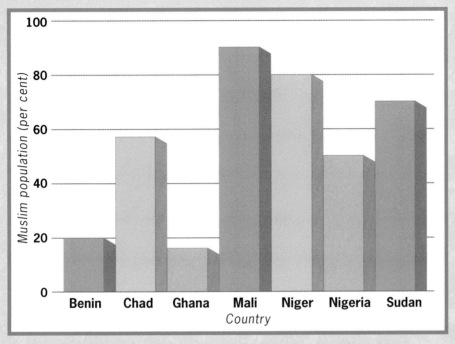

This graph shows the Muslim population (per cent) within selected African countries.

Through those years the war continued, but neither side looked capable of winning an outright victory. In the process the south's economy was all but destroyed, and the resulting famines claimed hundreds of thousands of lives. Both sides were guilty of serious breaches of **human rights**, including the sale of captives into slavery. By the time a peace deal was struck in 2002, the overall death toll had probably exceeded 2 million.

Nigeria
Africa's most populous country (approaching 120 million in 2002) is divided almost equally between Muslims and non-Muslims. In Nigeria it was the non-Muslims who fell out in the early years of independence. When the Ibos of the south-east tried to leave Nigeria and create a new state called Biafra, the Yorubas of the south-west joined with the Muslim Hausa of the north to stop them. Once this civil war (1967–70) was over, great efforts were

made to play down tribal differences and strengthen national unity. For most of the next 30 years the issues dividing Muslims and non-Muslims became less important than issues of economic development and administration, as Nigeria see-sawed alarmingly between **military dictatorships** and democratically–elected governments.

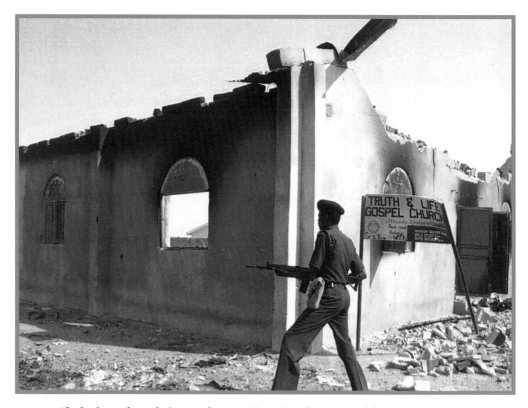

A Christian church in Kaduna, Nigeria, destroyed by rioting Muslims in February 2000.

However, as the century drew to a close there were signs that religious divisions were again coming to the fore. Sharia law was introduced in many of Nigeria's northern states, a development which many southern Nigerians found threatening. There were several large-scale religious clashes, one of which, in the northern city of Jos in September 2002, claimed over 500 lives.

Some experts argued that the roots of this violence were economic rather than religious, that there were simply too many young men in Nigeria without jobs or prospects. Many of these young men were justifiably angry, and religious extremism gave them the opportunity to express their anger.

Chad

In population terms, Chad is divided almost equally between the large, thinly-populated, Muslim north and the small, more thickly-populated, non-Muslim south. Those from the south, who mostly belong to the Sara **tribe**, were favoured by the French colonial rulers and inherited the government when independence was granted in 1960. When this government tried to impose its authority on the Muslim tribes of the north, however, the tribes rose in rebellion. By 1968 the situation was so bad that the government invited the French back to restore order. Once this was achieved, the government, rather than seeking reconciliation and real national unity, chose to **persecute** its Muslim citizens. By the mid-1970s the north was once more in open revolt, and for the next twelve years the country endured a series of civil wars punctuated by occasional ceasefires and foreign interventions by France, the USA and, most blatantly of all, Libya.

During these twelve years the original dispute between Muslims and non-Muslims was gradually overshadowed by disputes between the different Muslim tribes. It was fighting between these tribes which virtually destroyed the capital N'djamena and set back the country's hopes of economic development. Since 1990 Chad has mostly been at peace, and the recent discovery of significant oil reserves has given the country a chance to break free from the grip of its past.

Soldiers of Chad's civil war, July 1984.

Cold War victims: the Horn of Africa

Between 1947 and 1989 the USA and the Soviet Union competed with each other across the globe in what was known as the **Cold War**. This competition took many forms: political, cultural, economic, military and scientific. The two sides never actually came to blows with each other – their possession of nuclear weapons made that too dangerous – but they often sought to improve their global position by encouraging their friends and dependants to do so. Sometimes the two **superpowers** tried to use the developing world countries as positive examples of how their own systems worked. But more often than not they put their energies into undermining each other's dependants. As far as Africa was concerned, their competition was almost completely destructive.

Men, women and children are fed porridge and milk at a relief station in Ethiopia, during the famine of 1984-5.

The Horn of Africa (which now composes Ethiopia, Eritrea, Somalia and the small state of Djibouti) interested the superpowers because of its strategic position, alongside the

Red Sea oil route from the Middle East to Europe. The USA began supporting Ethiopia (which then included Eritrea) with lavish military aid in 1953, despite the fact that the governing regime of Emperor Haile Selassie was **corrupt** and inefficient. The regime's hatred of **communism** was reason enough for the USA. When neighbouring Somalia became independent in 1960, the Soviets offered help and friendship as a way of counteracting US influence in Ethiopia, and when the Somali military took power in 1969 the Soviets stepped up this support. They also offered assistance to the Eritreans, who had launched a struggle for independence from Ethiopia in 1961. Each superpower's support was largely military. A region of the world that desperately needed economic assistance was instead overflowing with weaponry.

Swapping sides

In 1974 a single event turned the whole region upside down. The US-supported government in Ethiopia, which had carried on holding banquets while 200,000 of its citizens starved in the famine of 1972-3, was suddenly overthrown by a group of military officers, most of whom had communist sympathies. This group launched a reign of terror against anyone else who dared to oppose them. By 1977 one man, Mengistu Haile Mariam, had emerged as the leader of the ruling committee or Dergue.

By this time, the USA had left, and Ethiopia's enemies had made the most of the Dergue's murderous in-fighting. Eritrean **guerrillas** had almost evicted the Ethiopians from Eritrea, and Somalia had launched a war to conquer the Ogaden, a vast region of south-eastern Ethiopia that the Somalis claimed was theirs. The Dergue asked their fellow-communists in the Soviet Union for help, and the Soviets, deciding that Ethiopia was a better long term bet than Somalia or Eritrea, promptly switched allies. Over the next three years Soviet advisers helped Mengistu retake most of Eritrea and all of the Ogaden. The USA, meanwhile, poured arms into Somalia.

There were many direct casualties of these wars, but many more indirect casualties. Money spent on weaponry could not be spent on agricultural development, and resources used to repair war damage could not be used for expansion. The region's economies, already staggering from the effects of the 1970s **world recession**, were brought to their knees by these overlapping wars, and the region's ordinary people found their lives becoming harder and more uncertain.

The Live Aid concert at London's Wembley Stadium was held in 1985 to help the victims of the Ethiopian famine.

Music Aid

In October 1984 a BBC news film about a famine in Ethiopia horrified millions of viewers. One of them was Bob Geldof, then the lead singer of the Boomtown Rats pop group. In November he and Ultravox singer Midge Ure wrote the song 'Do They Know It's Christmas?' and recorded it as *Band Aid* with a large group of British music celebrities. In January 1985 US stars followed suit, banding together as *USA for Africa* to record 'We Are The World'. Both these records, and the Live Aid concerts in London and Philadelphia, which followed that summer, raised huge sums of money for the charities working to save people from starvation in Ethiopia.

Downward spiral

The region's governments grew more brutal as they struggled to cope. This, in turn, created more violent opposition. By the end of the 1980s Ethiopia's Mengistu regime was losing its war in Eritrea and facing a formidable military challenge from the Tigray Liberation Front, an army formed in Ethiopia's northernmost province. In 1989 the **Cold War** ended, and the Soviets washed their hands of the regime they had done so much to promote. Two years later the Tigreans drove the Dergue from power, and two years after that Eritrea proclaimed its independence.

Somalia, meanwhile, was falling to pieces. Unlike many African countries it had only one major **ethnic** group, but this was divided into hostile **clans**. In the 1980s, with the country already awash with Soviet and American weapons, the Dergue and its Soviet allies did their best to stir up hatred between these clans.

By 1990 **civil war** was raging throughout Somalia, and many towns had been reduced to rubble. As the four major clans fought each other, so the central government became increasingly irrelevant and finally non-existent. **Refugees** poured across the borders in search of food, shelter and safety.

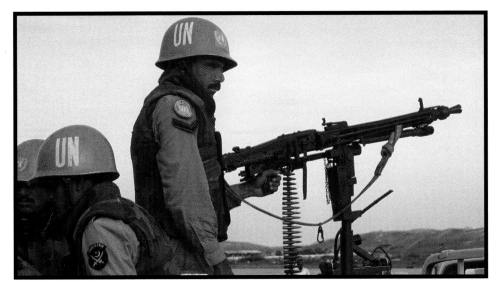

United Nations troops patrol the streets of the Somali capital Mogadishu in 1992.

The Somali economy collapsed, leaving famine in its wake. In 1992 **United Nations** (UN) troops were sent to maintain order while the famine relief agencies did their job. They suffered serious casualties in violent clashes with the Somali clans. (One of the clashes was turned into a Hollywood film, *Black Hawk Down.*) In 1994, with the famine under control, the UN withdrew its forces, and Somalia returned to chaos. Since then all efforts to create a new central government have failed.

A self-destructive habit

In 1998 Ethiopia and Eritrea went to war again, this time over a small, disputed strip of virtually worthless land. Eighty-five thousand people were killed, and over half a million refugees fled their homes. A **ceasefire** was signed in July 2000, and both sides agreed to accept the verdict of an independent border commission. Time will tell whether they mean it. In the Horn of Africa the conflicts provoked and encouraged by the Cold War superpowers have become almost self-sustaining, a self-destructive habit which the politicians and soldiers of the region seem unable to break.

Cold War victims: Angola

The other major African victim of the **Cold War** was Angola. The Portuguese had refused to give up their **colonial** possessions when the other European powers relinquished theirs in the late 1950s and early 1960s, but in 1974 the cost of keeping them provoked a revolution in Portugal itself. The new Portuguese government offered its three colonies a swift transition to independence. In both Portuguese Guinea and Mozambique there was only one major resistance movement to inherit power, but in Angola there were three: the Popular Movement for the Liberation of Angola (MPLA), the National Front for the Liberation of Angola (FLNA) and the National Union for Total Independence of Angola (UNITA). Each was based on a particular **tribe** (the Kimbundu, Bakongo and Ovimbundu, respectively), and each was supported by one of the **superpowers** (the MPLA by the Soviets, the other two by the USA). The Portuguese tried to persuade them to share power, but failed. As independence and **civil war** loomed, the Soviets and Americans began arming their clients.

First moves

From the outset the Soviet-supported MPLA controlled the capital, Luanda, and Angola's main source of income, the Cabinda oil wells. This gave it a clear economic advantage. The MPLA also had the more committed, more **idealistic** supporters, which gave it a political and military advantage. By November 1975 the MPLA had effectively destroyed the FNLA and forced the UNITA fighters back into the empty south-east of the huge country. The USA, who had only just lost their long war in Vietnam (1965–75), were reluctant to get involved in a similar conflict in Africa and stopped helping UNITA.

But UNITA was not finished. The **white minority government** in South Africa, worried that a pro-Soviet government in Angola would threaten both itself and the other white minority regimes in neighbouring Southern Rhodesia and South-West Africa (later Zimbabwe and Namibia), came to the rescue. They offered the UNITA leader Jonas Savimbi all the financial and military help he needed to keep the war going.

War by proxy

For the first ten years, until around 1987, UNITA's campaign was more of an annoyance than a threat to President dos Santos's MPLA government. The Soviets offered some economic help,

Cuban troops helped train the army, and the government pushed ahead with its **communist** programme. Its education and health reforms were much-needed and popular, but the government's method of copying inappropriate Soviet economic policies – taking many banks, industries and farms into state ownership – produced muddle and inefficiency. Ultimately this deprived the country of the money it needed to pay for the education and health programmes. As the war with UNITA continued, eating up money on arms and deterring foreign investors, the government became increasingly dependent on Angola's oil wealth to keep itself afloat.

UNITA had few real supporters. Savimbi's organization was a brutal **dictatorship** that condemned women opponents as witches and burnt them alive. It raised some of the money it needed by selling Angola's diamonds on the international market, but mostly relied on the financial help which it received from the South Africans and, eventually, the Americans. By the mid-1980s the Reagan administration in Washington was scenting victory in the Cold War, and was eager to take on the Soviets wherever it found them.

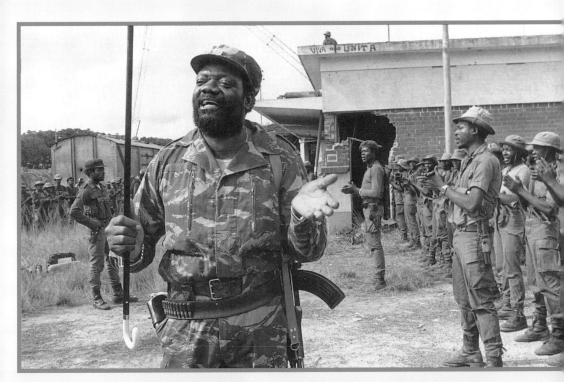

UNITA leader Jonas Savimbi shares a song with some of his troops at a station on Angola's Benguela Railway, April 1986.

By 1987 the war was turning in UNITA's favour, and more Cuban troops were needed to stem the tide. This upsurge in fighting did more damage to the economy, and the end of the **Cold War** in 1990 meant that the MPLA would soon have to survive without Soviet and Cuban help. Fortunately for the MPLA, South Africa was also under pressure to withdraw from the conflict, and in 1991 an agreement was reached. Both the Cubans and the South Africans would leave Angola, and nationwide elections would be held under **UN** supervision. Both Savimbi and the Americans were confident that UNITA would win the election – the Ovimbundu were, after all, Angola's largest tribe – but they didn't take into consideration Savimbi's reputation for brutality, and the fact that many Angolans blamed him for the length of the war. In September 1992 the MPLA won a majority in the assembly and dos Santos beat Savimbi for the presidency.

'Blood diamonds'

Over half the world's diamonds are found in Africa. Control of their excavation and sale has become a key element in many of Africa's most crippling wars. Easy to transport, hard to trace and simple to convert into cash, diamonds have become the most popular way of paying for the soldiers and weaponry that have terrorized countries like Angola, Liberia, Sierra Leone and the Congo. Just as money paid out for killings has earned the name 'blood money', so the diamonds used to finance Africa's wars have become known as 'blood diamonds'.

The final chapter

The USA admitted that the elections had been 'generally free and fair', but Savimbi refused to recognize the result. In October 1992 he tried and failed to seize power through a **coup** in the capital Luanda, and in January 1993 he restarted the civil war. Towns throughout the country were besieged by UNITA forces, and the war entered its most terrible phase. By mid-1993 over 1000 people a day were dying in battles, sieges or the famine spread by war. Between 10–15 million landmines had been sown across the country, and 100,000 Angolans had already lost at least one limb. The *New York Times* reporter John Darnton discovered one small town where 20,000 people, half of them children, were living on a diet of boiled insects and leaves.

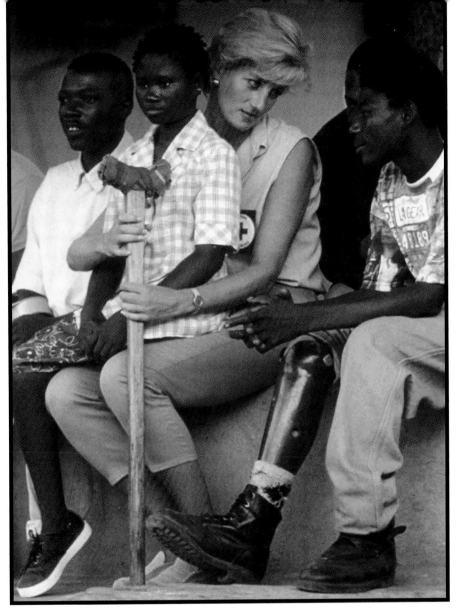

Princess Diana talks to Angolan victims of landmines at an orthopaedic workshop in the capital Luanda, 1997.

In 1994 the tide turned in favour of the MPLA government, and Savimbi would never again come so close to victory. He had lost his American backers – now that the Cold War was over Washington had drastically reduced its interest in African affairs. In 1995 Savimbi accepted the role of vice-president in a unified government, but then failed to turn up when the government was sworn in. In 1998 he once again restarted the war and the violence continued until a peace deal was finally struck in 2002. Savimbi himself was killed in February 2002.

Thieves and murderers

The legacies of slavery and **colonialism**, the harsh economic realities imposed by Western corporations and financial institutions, and the destructive impact of the **Cold War** all made life difficult for most African countries and their governments. But these governments were not completely powerless. They usually had some money to spend, and the chance to borrow more. A few African governments did their best to use what resources they possessed for the good of all their people: Tanzania under Julius Nyerere was a good example. Most African governments said they wanted to help their own people, but many were just as interested in enriching themselves. A small number went even further, abandoning all responsibility for the welfare of the people they ruled and helping themselves to whatever they could. These governments looted their own countries, and murdered anyone foolish or courageous enough to object.

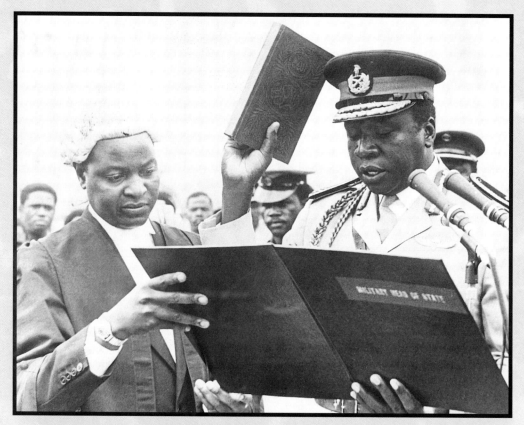

Idi Amin is sworn in as Uganda's new head of state in February 1971. During his eight years in power he tortured and murdered thousands of political opponents.

Idi Amin

Independent Uganda's first leader was Milton Obote. His nine years in office were marked by increasing heavy-handedness, economic inefficiency and **tribal** favouritism. In January 1971 he was overthrown by the head of the country's armed forces, Major-General Idi Amin Dada. Amin strengthened his position by killing those soldiers who came from tribes and Ugandan regions other than his own, and by employing large numbers of **mercenaries** from neighbouring countries. He and his new elite spent the next eight years plundering the country and killing anyone who opposed them.

Cashing in on power

During Idi Amin's rule in Uganda, planes loaded with luxury goods for Amin and his supporters – cars, jewellery, audio and video equipment, fine wines and spirits – frequently left the UK's Stansted Airport for the Ugandan capital, Kampala. The regularity of these flights earned them a nickname – 'The Stansted Shuttle'.

In 1972 Amin expelled all those South Asians who had settled in Uganda during the period of British colonial rule, and divided up their property and contracts between his supporters. Since the supporters had no experience of running such businesses, most of them collapsed, and by 1978 the country's economy had halved in size. Amin also set up a notorious security and intelligence force called the State Research Bureau. This force tortured and murdered as many as half a million Ugandans. Most were ordinary people, but Amin's victims included ministers, archbishops and even his own wife.

In September 1978 he made the mistake of attacking neighbouring Tanzania, probably with the intention of distracting his own people's attention from their economic problems. The Tanzanians pushed Amin's army back across the border, and reached the Uganda capital Kampala in the spring of 1979. Amin fled abroad, but many of his supporters retreated into the more inaccessible regions of the Ugandan countryside and continued their reign of terror.

Obote returned to power but repeated his earlier mistakes. In 1986 he was replaced by Yoweni Museveni, who began the daunting process of repairing and restoring those parts of the country that the central government controlled. He made much progress over the next sixteen years, but rebellions continued in the north and west, now led by the so-called Lord's Resistance Army. This claimed to follow the Bible's Ten Commandments, but specialized in kidnapping young girls for its leaders.

Joseph Mobutu in 1961, before he became president of the Congo.

Mobutu

When the Belgian Congo was granted independence in 1960 there were great hopes for the new country's future. Although the Belgians had done nothing to prepare the country for independence, there were huge reserves of cobalt, diamonds and copper. New hydro-electric dams on the Congo River had the potential to supply all the energy central Africa needed. Yet by the end of the century the country was deep in debt, its **infrastructure** in complete disrepair. Disease was rampant, unemployment running at 60 per cent, and **inflation** at 30 per cent. For the last twenty years the economy had been in virtual freefall.

The responsibility for this state of affairs rested with one man. Mobutu Sese Seko liked to call himself 'Papa', or the nation's 'Founder and Guide'. He came to power in 1965, after five years of intervention by Cold War rivals had worsened existing tribal animosities and destroyed any chances of a government that represented all the people. Mobutu attacked the colonial past and encouraged pride in African heritage. He changed his name from Joseph Mobutu to Mobutu Seso Seko and renamed the country Zaire, replacing European city and town names with African ones. He imprisoned or executed his enemies, and installed his friends in power. He denounced **communism** at every opportunity, which kept him on good terms with the USA and France. Both countries sent forces to save him from his own people in the late 1970s.

The country earned money from the sale of its minerals, and received substantial loans and aid from Western financial institutions. Mobutu and his friends pocketed most of it. The dictator had luxury homes in several European countries and many Congolese provinces; he travelled the world with a huge entourage, staying at the best hotels and shopping at the most exclusive stores. Money not spent was squirreled away in Swiss bank accounts, where the sums ran into billions of US dollars. Mobutu's regime even gave rise to a new word: just as people with a compulsion to steal are known as kleptomaniacs, so regimes which can't stop looting their own countries are now called 'kleptocracies'.

Bokassa

In 1966 the Central African Republic was taken over by its army leader, Jean-Bedel Bokassa. He declared himself president-for-life, and then proclaimed himself emperor of the new 'Central African Empire'. During his fourteen years in power he treated the whole country as if it were his personal property. Bokassa filled his luxurious palace with gold and diamonds, and killed whoever he felt like killing. Some enemies were dropped in the River Ubangi for the crocodiles, others were reportedly cooked and served up to visiting foreigners.

His coronation ceremony, modelled on Napoleon's in 1804, cost the country everything it earned from export sales in a whole year. French governments supported him for years, but finally decided he had gone too far when scores of children were clubbed to death in 1979. French forces overthrew him, and his successors put him on trial. A death sentence was reduced to life imprisonment, and Bokassa eventually died in 1996. The Central African Republic is still struggling to recover from his years in power.

Jean-Bedel Bokassa, the self-styled Emperor of Central Africa, at his coronation in 1977.

Turning point: 1970s – oil prices rise

The conflicts discussed in previous pages all took hold in the 1960s or early 1970s, when the rest of the African continent was still in the friendlier grip of post-independence optimism. Many of the new African governments managed to stay out of the **Cold War** and cope with the **tribal** and/or religious tensions that afflicted their countries. They prevented the concentration of power in the hands of brutal dictators and their supporters. For most of these governments, the development strategy of increasing exports and borrowing to fund a growing, more diversified economy, seemed to be working. An average growth rate of around 3 per cent was achieved in the 1960s, and this, though far from high, seemed a good first step on the road to development. Africa and its politicians had come some way towards meeting the expectations of independence.

New oil pipelines in Nigeria, October 1965. The country's huge oil reserves have played a vital role in keeping the economy afloat.

African countries are hit hard

By the end of the 1970s these hopes had been dashed. In 1973, and again in 1979, the price of crude oil soared; raising the cost of a barrel by 20 times. The causes of this price explosion had nothing to do with Africa, but its effects were a particular disaster for the continent. Only a handful of **sub-Saharan African** countries had energy supplies of their own, and the rest relied on imported oil for between 60 and 90 per cent of their energy needs. Development plans designed around cheap oil now had to be rewritten. Each extra pound spent on imported oil was one pound less to invest in the future.

There was more bad news. In the developed West, higher oil prices made industrial goods more expensive to produce and transport, so African countries found they were paying more for these as well. At the same time, the world economic slowdown that followed the oil price rises meant that the Western economies wanted less of the raw materials which Africa sold. The price of these went down. African governments were hit both ways. As less money flowed in, more flowed out.

Three other factors played a part in making things even worse. The spread of Western medical knowledge was one of **colonialism's** more welcome contributions to Africa, but even this had its down-side: thanks to better health-care, the population was now growing at over 3 per cent per annum. Food production, on the other hand, was not growing at anything like that speed. Most of the newly-independent governments had made a point of encouraging their farmers to grow crops for export, not for food. They had also welcomed the drift to the towns, thinking that the new industries and services would need workers, but overlooking the fact that they also needed food. By the 1980s many African countries were spending more and more of their diminishing income on importing food that they could have grown themselves.

Terms of trade

*'Throughout Africa the story is the same. Africa is in debt. Because it must reduce spending, it cannot build up its **infrastructure** to compete with industrialised nations. It cannot control the price paid for its exports, which keep falling. It cannot determine the price it pays for goods it must import, which keep rising. It wants fair trade ... In theory, Africa is free to trade: in practice, it faces immense problems.'*
From Africa in Crisis, an educational pack put together by the Save The Children charity organization

Finally, there was a growing problem of debt. As governments found it harder and harder to balance their budgets, so the temptation was to borrow more and more. Year by year the interest on the loans mounted up. By 1982 Mobutu's Zaire needed two thirds of its annual income just to pay the interest on that year's debt and what was still owed from the previous year.

Unhelpful aid

By the 1980s Africa was in dire need of economic help, but little meaningful assistance was given. Western people gave generously in crisis situations like the Ethiopian famine of 1984–5, but their governments were nothing like as helpful. They gave the Africans weapons, and money which had to be spent on goods from their own countries, even when these goods could be bought more cheaply elsewhere. Such aid tended to be more profitable for the giver than the receiver.

A father and his two children at the Korem aid centre in Ethiopia during the famine of 1984–85.

The international institutions that had been set up by the **UN** – the International Bank for Reconstruction and Development (the World Bank) and the International Monetary Fund (the IMF) – were prepared to lend the Africans more money, but only on terms acceptable to the Western countries that supplied the funds. African countries were asked to stop subsidizing food prices for their poor, and to reduce health and education services that their economies could not really afford. They were also told to 'free up' their economies, which meant removing any health and safety restrictions, or any **trade union** powers to protect wages, which might deter Western companies from investing in their countries.

Economic inequality within Africa becomes even more severe in times of crisis. While some maintain a relatively high standard of living, hundreds of thousands, like these Kenyans in Nairobi, live in poverty.

These conditions were bound to impoverish further ordinary Africans, and to widen the gap between them and the elites who ruled them. Some African governments, less concerned with their people's well-being than the maintenance of their own privileged lifestyles, accepted the conditions willingly. Others did so with considerable reluctance. But most gave in.

Things fall apart

This change of economic direction had obvious political consequences. Ordinary Africans noticed that their governments continued to live well while their own lives got harder and harder, and they grew increasingly angry. The expectations of independence were no longer being met, and their own governments seemed at least partly to blame. These African governments were within reach, unlike the foreign governments and corporations who took so many of the decisions that affected African lives.

Many of the governments sought to deflect their people's anger on to others. Unable to blame their Western backers, these governments sought out **scapegoats** at home, often picking on the representatives of other tribes. These tribes fought back, and incidents of violence multiplied. As Africa's economy shrank, more than a few of its nations began to unravel.

31

West African civil wars

During the final decade of the 20th century two West African states were virtually destroyed by **civil wars** of dreadful ferocity. These two conflicts, in Liberia and Sierra Leone, had very similar causes and followed remarkably similar paths. As such, they offered a vivid and frightening picture of where much of Africa was heading if the continent's economy was allowed to collapse.

Master-Sergeant Samuel K. Doe, who seized the presidency of Liberia in 1980.

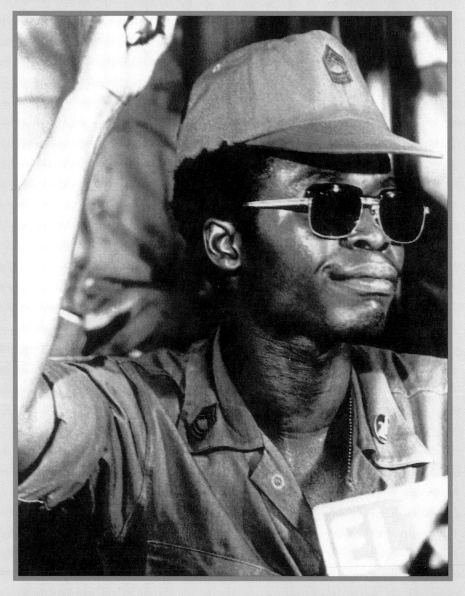

End of a regime

The event that triggered civil war in Liberia was a government attempt, in April 1979, to raise the price of rice – which formed a large part of most ordinary Liberians' diet – by 50 per cent. Massive riots were followed by harsh repression, and repression by a military **coup**. In April 1980 the group that had ruled Liberia for a century and a half was overthrown by seventeen low-ranking soldiers led by Master-Sergeant Samuel Doe. All the old government leaders were executed. Thirteen of them were tied to posts on the beach and shot in front of the television cameras. Free elections, a new **constitution** and economic justice were promised. None were delivered.

The only real difference between the new regime and the old was that a different tribal group was now in power. Doe's **tribe** – the Krahns – were given all the important posts; any outspoken opponents were imprisoned and, more often than not, tortured and killed. The regime lived off the sale of diamonds and its share of the US-owned Firestone Rubber Corporation's profits. The rest of the economy, and the living standards of ordinary Liberians, were allowed to collapse.

Death of a country

On Christmas Eve of 1989 an army led by Charles Taylor invaded the country from bases in neighbouring Guinea. His troops were mostly from the Gio and Mano tribes, who together made up about a sixth of Liberia's population. Many were still children, and these were often given alcohol or drugs to make them less afraid. Over the next eight months Taylor's troops burned, raped and murdered their way across the country, reducing Doe's soldiers to a foothold on the coast and encouraging the birth of other armies representing other tribes.

In August 1990 a West African Multilateral Force involving troops from Nigeria, Ghana, Guinea, Sierra Leone and the Gambia tried to restore order and failed. Doe died a horrible death at the hands of one rebel army, but none of them was able to seize overall control of the country. For the next seven years Liberia and its people were ravaged by up to six tribally-based armies, each intent on wiping out their **tribal** enemies. By 1994 over 150,000 people had been killed, or 5 per cent of the population. A similar percentage of the UK population would number about 3 million.

The other West African states continued with their efforts, and these, along with a general war-weariness, finally led to elections in July 1997. These were won by Charles Taylor, mostly because Liberians knew he would restart the war if he lost. For two years there was relative peace, but a new rebellion began in 1999, and by 2002 Taylor's rule was under serious threat. Liberia, like Somalia, had become virtually ungovernable.

Child soldiers

At the end of the 21st century there were said to be around 300,000 soldiers, operating in 30 countries, who had not yet reached their 18th birthdays. The fact that modern weapons are light and easy to operate has encouraged the (often forced) recruitment of children in many wars. Since 1994 a UN working group has been trying to create new international rules forbidding the recruitment of child soldiers.

'I joined when I was 13 years old. I was just forced to fight because I was separated from my parents and the rest of my family. I had to fight for my own survival. I was given six months of training and became a special forces member. I fought on the front lines, but I wasn't afraid the first time because I had been given drugs. I fired a mortar. I experienced some terrible things during the war. I saw some terrible things and did some terrible things. I saw people being killed, I saw fighters eat people's hearts. They burned people and killed young babies. I did these things too because we had to obey orders. After the war, I tried to find my family, but they have disappeared. So now I live near a road-side store. That's where I live and sleep.
I am haunted by what we did during the war ... I have lost my ability to feel. You can cut me with a knife and I won't even feel it. I cry but only when I'm happy.'
A child soldier from Liberia tells his story, taken from the Radio Netherlands Human Rights internet site. (In 1997 this boy, Tom, was given a place on a carpentry course, where he learned how to make furniture.)

Liberians flee from their country's civil war on a Nigerian cargo ship, May 1996.

Repeat prescription

The civil war in Sierra Leone began in 1991, two years after the beginning of civil war in Liberia. As in Liberia, there was massive dissatisfaction among the population as a whole. Falling world prices for agricultural products and the inefficiency of local politicians had led to a dramatic decline in ordinary living standards, but those same local politicians continued to prosper, thanks to their control of the country's diamond, bauxite and titanium mines. In March 1991 a group calling itself the Revolutionary United Front (RUF) began an armed rebellion. Three years of butchery and destruction later, the RUF and its leader Foday Sankoh were in control of the country's mines.

The weakened central government was overthrown by a military coup, elections were held, and the winner overthrown by another coup. Several armies were now fighting each other, and another West African Multilateral Force was sent in. The elected government was reinstated, but lasted less than a year. In early 1999 RUF soldiers took over Freetown, maiming and murdering thousands of women, children and old people. Much of the city was burnt down. By this time the country's economy had collapsed, and half the country's people had fled their homes. By 2000, however, Foday Sankoh had been captured, and a permanent settlement seemed to be developing.

Turning point: Genocide in Rwanda

The two previous turning points in Africa's modern history had their origins outside the continent. Independence was, in most cases, given rather than taken, and the economic crisis that took root in the late 1970s grew out of a **world recession**. The **genocide** in Rwanda had roots in both colonial history and the economic crisis of the 1980s, but it was committed by Africans against Africans. The initial crime against humanity was terrible enough in itself, but it also triggered a wider war in central Africa that eventually involved half a dozen other African states and may have cost as many as 3 million lives.

The power of hatred

Rwanda is a small, fertile country with a large population; 90 per cent are Hutus, the other 10 per cent mostly Tutsis. The two peoples share the same language and much of the same culture, but they have long been traditional enemies, both here and in neighbouring Burundi. The Belgian **colonial** rulers reinforced this hostility by favouring the Tutsis at the Hutus' expense, giving them the best administrative jobs and business contracts.

After independence the Hutus took power, and there was massive discrimination against the once-dominant Tutsis, many of whom moved to neighbouring Uganda, Burundi and Zaire. In 1990 these Tutsi exiles, who now numbered well over half a million, formed their own army, the Rwandese Patriotic Front (RPF), with the intention of eventually returning to reclaim their lost lands and rights. The Hutu government in Rwanda, led by President Juvénal Habyarimana, expanded its own army with French help. All-out war between the two **tribes** seemed imminent.

By this time the Rwandan economy, like most African economies, was in bad shape. Coffee exports supplied 75 per cent of the country's income, and the price of coffee on the world market had collapsed. The country's population, meanwhile, had grown at a rapid rate. There were more mouths to feed, but less money to buy food.

The international community was willing to help Rwanda, but only if the government sorted out the tribal conflict that was threatening to tear the country apart. Habyarimana agreed in principle to multi-party elections and the merging of his Hutu army with the Tutsi RPF, but his own supporters prevented him from keeping these promises. He was returning to the Rwandan capital Kigali on 6 April 1994 when his plane was shot down, almost certainly by his former supporters in the *Interahamwe*, the semi-official Hutu militia whose name means 'those who stand together'. For them, fear and hatred of the Tutsis were more important than Rwanda's economic well-being.

Genocide

Before the assassination was even announced on the radio, the *Interahamwe* squads had begun killing Habyarimana's Hutu supporters and any Tutsis they could find. Fictional reports of Tutsi attacks were broadcast on the state radio and Hutus told to defend themselves. At the same time orders were passed down through government channels for the mass murder of the Tutsis. The authorities in each town, each village, were told that only the complete elimination of the Tutsis – men, women, children and babies – would guarantee their own safety. These authorities handed out weapons and told their people where to find the Tutsis. Any who protested were themselves threatened or killed.

The bodies of Tutsis, massacred by Hutus, lie outside a Rwandan church, 1994.

The terrified Tutsis ran for their lives, but few escaped. Those who sought sanctuary in churches or hospitals were either dragged out and killed or burnt to death inside the buildings. Over the next hundred days around a million Tutsis were murdered by Hutu armed groups and mobs.

Terror

*'Our sector was attacked on the night of the 10th [April].
We watched as our houses were burned down and our
cows stolen and eaten ... [We fled] towards the Adventist
church of Muhomboli ...*

*'On the 13th, we saw an enormous group of militia ... They
surrounded the church ... They threw grenades through
the windows and doors which they managed to break
down. Once they overcame all resistance from the refugees
they entered the church. I saw that death was waiting for
me. I pretended to be dead and listened to the movement
of the killers as I lay underneath numerous corpses ...'*
**Justin Kanamugire, a 32-year-old Tutsi farmer, quoted in
African Rights, Rwanda: Death, Despair and Defiance
(London, 1995)**

Aftermath

The Tutsi RPF invaded from Uganda, and by early July had
captured Kigali. As the Tutsi troops fanned out across the
country more than a million Hutus fled westwards, over the
Zairean border.

**UN troops evacuate Hutu survivors of a massacre committed by the
(mostly Tutsi) Rwandan Army, April 1995.**

Inside Rwanda a government was set up that included both Tutsis and Hutus, and order was slowly restored. The USA, still stinging from its failure in Somalia, refused to sanction the sending of a **UN** peacekeeping force, but French troops created a **'safety zone'** in south-west Rwanda for those Hutus who wished to return.

Rwandan refugees on the march in November 1996 during Africa's 'Great War', as the central African conflict came to be called.

The **refugee** camps across the Zairean border were over-crowded, unsanitary and poorly-supplied. These camps were home to the worst of the *Interahamwe* killers, who over the next few years would usually be called the **genocidaires**. Few were in favour of helping such men, but they had guns, so they ran the camps. As aid poured in from the international relief agencies the Hutu genocidaires recovered their strength. Within a year they were ready to threaten the peace once more, in both their old home of Rwanda and their new home, Mobutu's Congo.

Seeking justice

Late in 1994 a UN Tribunal was set up in Arusha, Tanzania, to try those suspected of playing a leading role in the Rwandan genocide. Many of the wanted men were hard to find, evidence was often difficult to obtain and confirm, and progress was extremely slow. By 2000 only seven verdicts had been handed down by the UN-appointed judges. Since then, several more suspects have been flushed out of their European and US hiding places and sent back to Arusha, but it seems unlikely that the principal authors and perpetrators of the genocide will ever stand trial.

Africa's 'Great War'

The **genocidaires** who dominated the **refugee** camps in eastern Zaire had no intention of spending their whole lives as refugees. Through 1995 and early 1996 they conducted military raids across the Rwandan border, built up their supply of weapons and sought allies for an eventual reconquest of their homeland. The Zairean government, which was fighting rebellious Tutsis on its own territory, and Ugandan rebels based in eastern Zaire, supported the genocidaires.

Fearing an invasion, the new Tutsi-dominated government in Rwanda formed alliances of its own: with Tutsi rebels in eastern Zaire, the Ugandan government, and Zairean rebels led by Laurent Kabila. The Tutsi government initially restricted themselves to arming and supporting these partners inside Zaire, but in October 1996 it took the final plunge and launched a full-scale invasion. Within days the refugee camps had been cleared. Some 700,000 Hutus fled back across the border to Rwanda; a further 400,000 – which included most of the genocidaires – retreated westward into the vast rain forests of Zaire. Rwanda's domestic nightmare had now become a war between, on the one side, the Tutsis and Kabila, on the other, the Hutu genocidaires and Mobutu.

Zairean rebel leader Laurent Kabila addresses some of his troops in February 1997. He became president in May of that year.

Round two

The next phase of the conflict proved shorter than most observers expected. Most of Mobutu's forces ran away from the invaders, looting villages and killing civilians as they fled. By May 1997 the Rwandan-supported rebels were approaching the Zairean capital Kinshasa. Mobutu escaped to Morocco, only to die of cancer soon afterwards. Laurent Kabila, who had been fighting him for over thirty years, took over the government. Zaire was renamed the Democratic Republic of the Congo.

It soon became apparent that Kabila was not much of an improvement on his predecessor. He snuffed out hopes of international help for his poverty-stricken country by insulting foreign diplomats and holding foreign businessmen to ransom. Rather than take sensible action to help the economy, he simply printed more money and made the situation worse. He also failed to reward his Rwandan backers by handing over the Hutu genocidaires. On the contrary, he employed them to protect his own government. Throughout those areas of the newly-named Congo that he controlled, Kabila behaved as **dictatorially** as Mobutu had done.

'It's our country'

'In Walungu Hospital, near Bukavu, 1200 patients compete for 300 beds, and the attention of three doctors. About half the inmates are relatively healthy, but too terrified to go back home. Murals in the hospital depict black doctors in white coats peering into microscopes, recalling the lost hopes of the 1960s. Now, the wards are full of black children with blonde hair, a sign of malnutrition. The hospital's 32-year-old head of nursing says she has received only three months' salary in her whole career. Why does she carry on? "It's our country," she shrugs. "It's painful, but there it is."'
Quoted in 'Africa's Great War', The Economist, 6 July 2002.

Kabila had supporters. The MPLA government in neighbouring Angola had never got on with Mobutu, because Mobutu had allowed UNITA to use Zairean territory as a safe base. Kabila, on the other hand, was more than willing to sacrifice UNITA in return for Angolan government support. The government of Robert Mugabe in Zimbabwe and Sam Nujoma's government in

Namibia also offered military help. In their cases the motives were more mixed: sympathy with Kabila, a distraction from domestic troubles, and greed for the Congo's mineral riches.

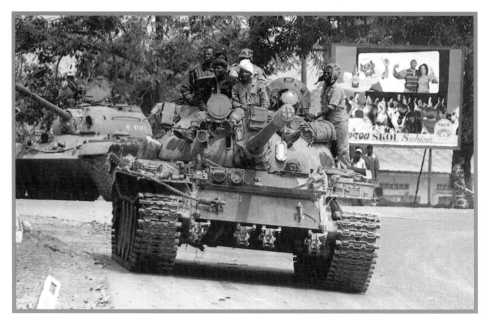

Congolese rebel forces head for the capital, Kinshasa, in August 1998, intent on overthrowing President Kabila.

Kabila's supporters, however, were no match for his enemies. Within a year of his installation as president, he had lost the eastern half of the Congo to various rebel armies supported by the Rwandans and Ugandans. In 1998 Rwanda sent its own 40,000-strong army – the best organized fighting force in Central Africa – across the border once more. The intention, as before, was to destroy the genocidaires and their Congolese protector. In 1996 the protector had been Mobutu. Now it was Kabila.

The 'Great War'

The Congo is a vast, heavily-forested country with few paved roads, few working telephones and many **tribes**. For one state to permanently restrain it was next to impossible, particularly when other states were keen to enter the dispute. Uganda offered the Rwandans support in the east; Angola and Zimbabwe sent forces to protect Kabila in the west. Namibia, Chad and Burundi also sent some troops to help one side or the other, if only briefly. The troubles of Rwanda had merged with the troubles of the Congo, and the troubles of the Congo had turned into what journalists began calling Africa's 'Great War'.

This term was somewhat misleading. Over the next four years the Congo was consumed by many loosely-connected minor wars, not one great battle between competing alliances. What little law and order still existed simply disintegrated, leaving the ordinary people at the mercy of whichever armed groups happened to be in the neighbourhood. The country was stripped bare. Its people were killed in their hundreds of thousands, many by soldiers, many more by the famine they brought in their wake.

There was no chance of anyone winning this war, but many chances to make a profit. The original motivations behind the various foreign incursions were varied. The Rwandan government had reason to dislike Kabila's support for the fugitive Hutus, and the Ugandans had similar concerns about Ugandan rebels using north-eastern Congo as a safe haven. The Angolan government was grateful to Kabila for shutting out UNITA, and feared that a different Congolese government might let them back in. Kabila himself asked the Zimbabweans for military protection.

The Zimbabweans agreed, but only in return for a share of Congolese diamond and cobalt profits. The greed of the other states involved was not, at first, quite so obvious, but as the war ground to a stalemate it became increasingly clear that all of them were effectively looting the country. One UN report criticized Uganda, Zimbabwe and Burundi for illegally exporting Congolese diamonds, copper, coltan, cobalt and gold. Another report listed some 30 Western companies who had conspired with them. As the 20th century ended, the Congo was like a house full of burglars, its wealth disappearing, its people in terror.

Congolese take the town of Sona Bata, 65 kilometres (40 miles) from Kinshasa, August 1998.

Independence: Forty years later

The violence and heart-wrenching misery that afflicted Somalia, Angola, Liberia, Sierra Leone and the Congo in the 1990s stole most of the headlines in world news bulletins, but there were 35 other states in **sub-Saharan Africa**, and most of these were struggling with similar problems. Unlike the five states listed above, they had not, as yet, been overwhelmed by them. But neither had they solved them.

Politics

The end of the **Cold War** had both positive and negative impacts on Africa. On the positive side, African states were no longer subject to **superpower** manipulation and interference. If one **tribe** was in power in a pro-Western country, the other tribes were not being stirred up and armed by the Soviets. And vice versa. On the negative side, countries were no longer being bribed with economic help to keep them loyal. The Africans had lost their chance to play one side off against the other. More seriously, the continent had become less important, less relevant, to the rest of the world.

One positive consequence was the spread of **democracy** that took place in the 1990s. At the beginning of that decade multi-party systems only existed in Botswana, the Gambia, Senegal, Zimbabwe and Namibia. Once the Cold War was over many Western governments and financial institutions started demanding moves towards democracy as a condition for giving aid. There was self-interest in this – democratic states tended to be more stable, and therefore offered greater security for Western investments – but it also made many African governments more accountable to their own peoples.

These political improvements were patchy, and sometimes cancelled out by a steady weakening of social values. In many countries 40 years of **corrupt** government had removed all respect for politicians and the law, and the stressing of tribal identities had reduced any sense of nationhood or wider humanity. The flood of **refugees** fleeing the continent's many wars had stretched African life support systems to the limit. Ordinary people had grown used to doing whatever they needed to do, and taking whatever they needed to take, in order to survive. In the sprawling **shanty towns** that ringed Africa's cities, crime was rampant.

Global warming

Over the last 30 years Africa has suffered from unusually severe climatic conditions. Drought struck at the Sahel (a region with little rainfall to the south of the Sahara) throughout the 1970s and 1980s, at Ethiopia, Somalia and Sudan at frequent intervals in the 1980s and 1990s, and southern Africa in the early 1990s. By contrast, Mozambique and Malawi faced torrential rains and widespread flooding in 2000–2001. Most experts believe that **global warming** – which is mostly caused by the burning of fossil fuels like oil and coal – has been responsible for these increasingly violent shifts in normal climactic patterns. Those same experts agree that the less developed countries will find it much harder to cope with the consequences of global warming, so Africa is likely to suffer more than most. Africans, of course, are quick to point out that global warming has, for the most part, been caused by the industries of the developed world.

Mozambicans in February 2000, trapped by rising floodwaters.

AIDS

The HIV/AIDS virus had, by the end of the century, infected over 25 million people in sub-Saharan Africa. In the year 2000 alone, 10,500 new cases were reported each day. This rapid spread of the virus, while obviously tragic for each and every victim, also threatened the whole economic future of the region.

Since HIV/AIDS is a sexually-transmitted disease, the portion of the population most at risk is that aged 15–45, the same portion responsible for building the economy. The World Bank announced in 2000 that the epidemic was at least partly to blame for the decline in Africa's already poor growth rate. If the disease is not quickly brought under control – something which at present seems highly unlikely – the continent seems to be heading for a human and economic catastrophe.

John Githinji Paul, a three-year-old with HIV/AIDS, rests in his bed at a home for AIDS orphans in Nairobi, Kenya, 2000.

Economics

The end of the Cold War had little impact on Africa's economic situation. The decline of the late 1970s and 1980s continued into the 1990s. Held down by debt, Western self-interest and the **corruption** of their own governments, only four of sub-Saharan Africa's 40 states managed a better than 2 per cent growth rate – the sort of rate all European and North American states took for granted – in the years 1987–97. The economies of 22 sub-Saharan states shrank rather than grew. Africa was sliding backwards.

The West African state of Ghana offered a good example of how things were going wrong. There was no **civil war** in Ghana, and the government during this period, though hardly democratic in the Western sense, was neither brutal nor particularly corrupt. Through the 1990s the country seemed to be making modest but steady progress, but in 2000 its economy was hit by a drastic fall in the world price of cocoa (one of its two main exports), an unusually low price for gold (the other chief export), and a two-fold increase in the price of its oil imports. There was nothing any Ghanaian government could do about this, other than hope for a change in their economic circumstances.

Africa was given notice of one welcome change in 1999. The Western governments, awash with the wealth amassed during a decade of excellent economic growth, announced that they were cancelling at least some of the debt owed by some African countries. The list of countries was expanded in both 2000 and 2001, and these **debt relief** measures were certainly welcomed by many African governments and peoples. They were, however, often less generous than they seemed, and in themselves did little to solve the basic problems afflicting the African economy. The West, while insisting that only free trade could help Africa, protected their own agriculture against African competition. What Africa needed was the opposite: permission to protect its own infant industries and unrestricted access to Western markets.

Three leaders

Since independence there has been a bewildering variety of African leaders. Many of them, like these three, have been prepared to break the laws of their own countries in order to seize and retain political power. Only a few African leaders, however, have gone on to give up their positions of power voluntarily – something these three men have also all done.

Jerry Rawlings: Ghana

Born in Accra, Ghana, in 1947, Jerry Rawlings became an officer in Ghana's post-independence air force. In June 1979 he led the group of junior officers that overthrew the last in a succession of **corrupt** military governments. After jailing or executing those he considered responsible for the **corruption**, Rawlings returned the country to civilian rule. Two years later, deciding that nothing had really changed, he seized power again. The **constitution** was suspended, political parties banned and measures introduced to increase the participation of ordinary Ghanaians in economic and political decision-making. The country's poor economic performance – mostly caused by Ghana's international situation, but not helped by Rawlings' policies – eventually forced a change of direction. An economic recovery programme was agreed with the IMF and World Bank, and **democracy** was slowly re-introduced. Rawlings won presidential elections in both 1992 and 1996 before standing down in 2000. Critics stressed his poor **human rights** records, while supporters argued that his rule had saved Ghana from corruption and serious **tribal** strife.

Jerry Rawlings.

Daniel arap Moi: Kenya

A member of Kenya's Kalenjin **ethnic** minority, Daniel arap Moi was born in 1924. He was appointed vice-president by Jomo Kenyatta, Kenya's first post-independence leader, in 1967. When Kenyatta died

Daniel arap Moi.

in 1978, Moi became president, a post he held until 2002. Like many African leaders he changed the political system to secure his position and increase his power, surrounded himself with members of his own tribe and helped himself to the nation's wealth. When corrupt and inefficient management worsened the country's existing economic problems, he sought to divert attention from his own failures by stirring up grievances between tribes. In the 1990s international and domestic pressure forced Moi to reintroduce democratic elections; in both 1992 and 1997 he triumphed over a tribally-divided opposition. However, the country's constitution forbade him from standing again in the December 2002 elections, and his chosen successor for the presidency, Jomo Kenyatta's son Uhuru, was soundly beaten. It remains to be seen whether the new president, Mwai Kibaki, whose supporters include many former supporters of Moi, will introduce any real economic and political changes.

Olusegun Obasanjo: Nigeria

Olusegun Obasanjo.

This Nigerian leader was born in 1937. A career soldier from the Yoruba tribe, Obasanjo headed the military government that took power in 1976. Three years later he became the first African military leader to hand power back to civilians, as he announced his retirement from politics. He was still considered a threat, however, and in 1995 he was imprisoned by the **dictatorial** Sani Abacha. When Abacha died in 1998, Obasanjo was persuaded to run for president. His victory convinced many that Nigeria had turned a vital corner, but over 10,000 Nigerians have died in violent ethnic clashes since 1998, and the country's economic woes have worsened. Obasanjo has been unwilling to tackle the root causes of these problems, and Nigeria's considerable oil wealth still disappears into too many private pockets. He knows that any serious attempt to tackle corruption would probably result in his overthrow, and he has also discovered that ordinary Nigerians will resist attacks on their living standards – fuel price rises in both 2000 and 2002 provoked **general strikes** and government climbdowns.

The Western media and Africa

On television news programmes Africa correspondents stand in front of burnt-out buildings, piles of corpses, hospital wards full of buzzing flies and dying children. The images are usually heart-rending, but rarely placed in context. Africa is portrayed almost exclusively as a disaster zone, but there is little attempt to explain why this should be the case. The other Africa, of ordinary people struggling, in often difficult circumstances, to simply get on with their lives, is rarely shown. A small country like Benin, which has been spared natural disasters, widespread human violence and is doing reasonably well, will never be seen or heard from. African news is calamity news.

A television crew arrives at a refugee camp in the eastern Congo during the Rwanda crisis of 1994.

The news media are not alone in sticking to **stereotype**. In Hollywood's earlier days movies set in Africa were about white men hunting game on the plains, crash-landing aircraft in the desert or swinging through trees in the rain forest. With a few honourable exceptions, they used Africa as an adventure playground, in which the native animals were considered more interesting than the native humans. In more recent times mainstream films have concentrated on colonial bravery (*Khartoum, Zulu*), wars involving white mercenaries (*The Dogs of War, The Wild Geese*), the struggle against white rule in South Africa (*Cry Freedom, Biko*), and the saving of African animal species from extinction (*Gorillas in the Mist*). Here too, Western audiences have been left in ignorance of the lives most Africans lead.

Forgotten continent

Perhaps the most telling factor about the media coverage of Africa is how little there actually is. Despite centuries of British involvement in Africa, despite the upsurge in African-American interest in the continent that grew out of the 1960s civil rights movement, news of African events is often hard to come by. The wars in Sudan and Angola dragged on for more than 30 years, but rarely received any attention, and when peace deals were struck in 2002 the media interest was minimal.

Those who run the media might argue that thousands of Europeans, North Americans and Australians visit **sub-Saharan Africa's** game parks and sites of outstanding natural beauty, yet very few of them choose to venture beyond, into the rest of Africa. However, if the fuller picture is not shown, the West will continue to think only of poverty, famine and disaster when thinking of Africa. Perhaps a more balanced portrayal would encourage more people to see the real Africa.

'Compassion without understanding'

'Where television is concerned, African news is generally only big news when it involves a lot of dead bodies. The higher the mound, the greater the possibility that the world will, however briefly, send its camera teams and correspondents. Once the story has gone 'stale' – i.e. there are no new bodies and the **refugees** *are down to a trickle – the news circus moves on. The powerful images leave us momentarily horrified but largely ignorant, what somebody memorably described as having "compassion without understanding."'*
Fergal Keane, from his first-hand account of the Rwandan genocide, Season of Blood, A Rwandan Journey **(Penguin, 1996)**

Turning point: 2002 – year of peace?

2002 brought some good news for Africa. Four of the continent's longest-running **civil wars** were brought to an end, at least temporarily. For many observers, long driven to despair by the continent's epidemic of violence, this multiple outbreak of peace seemed like a new dawn, as welcome as it was unexpected.

Giving peace a chance

In Sierra Leone, Foday Sankoh's horrific invasion of the capital Freetown in early 1999 was followed by an uneasy **ceasefire** and the dispatch of a **UN** peacekeeping force. In 2000 the war flared up again, and 1000 British troops were sent to stop Sankoh from retaking Freetown. The rebel leader was captured, and over the next two years the UN forces gradually extended their area of control. By early 2001 most of the rebels had been disarmed. The war was declared over in January 2002, and elections held in the following May. Much of the country was in ruins, but the previous levels of violence and fear had been dramatically reduced.

The Angolan civil war was tilted in the government's favour by UNITA's loss of its Zairean safe haven early in 1998. When UNITA's leader Jonas Savimbi was killed in a gun battle with government troops in February 2002, the heart and drive went out of the rebels. A ceasefire was agreed in April, and UNITA's army disbanded in August. After 27 years, and at least two million unnecessary deaths, the war seemed finally over.

In July 2002 the two sides in the Sudanese civil war managed, somewhat unexpectedly, to agree a 'framework deal' for peace. They would share power for six years, and at the end of that period the inhabitants of the three southern provinces would be allowed to vote for or against a separate state of their own.

In the same month a deal was struck to end Africa's 'Great War'. In 2001 Laurent Kabila had been assassinated by one of his bodyguards, and succeeded by his son Joseph. Though lacking in experience, Joseph Kabila had soon shown himself to be more interested in peace than his father. In July 2002 he and the Rwandans came to an agreement. In return for Kabila's promise to disarm and deport the Hutu **genocidaires**, Rwanda would withdraw its army from Congolese territory within 90 days.

After months of chaos, everyday activities have resumed for many in Sierra Leone. Now crowds flock to the fish markets.

Hopes and fears

Whether, or how long, these peace deals will last is far from clear. The success of the UN intervention in Sierra Leone surprised many observers, and much depends on how successful the newly-elected government proves in its attempts to reconstruct the country, both economically and psychologically.

The Sudanese peace deal was the least expected of the four, and was already fraying badly at the edges by the autumn of 2002. The fact that large reserves of oil have recently been discovered in the south makes it unlikely that the deal will stick. It is hard to imagine the **Muslim** north allowing the Christian south to walk away with most of Sudan's potential wealth.

Many observers were equally pessimistic about the deal to end the 'Great War', but the Rwandans kept their promise to withdraw their forces from eastern Congo within 90 days, and much now depends on whether Joseph Kabila's Congolese government can deliver on its side of the bargain.

The Johannesburg Earth Summit

In August and September 2002 a World Summit on Sustainable Development was held in Johannesburg, South Africa. Its main aims were the reduction of poverty throughout the less developed world – of which Africa formed such a large part – and increased protection for the environment. Important agreements were reached to halve the number of people with inadequate sanitation, reduce the use of harmful chemicals, maintain the number of fish in the seas and halt the extinction of plant and animal species. There was, however, less agreement on how these and other targets were to be achieved, and no way of forcing individual countries or corporations to take the steps that seemed necessary. A hundred world leaders addressed the Earth Summit, giving some hope for Africa's future. People are keen to try to find solutions to its many problems, and although the outcome at the Summit in Johannesburg did not produce any single momentous breakthrough, the results were more comprehensive than any previous outcome.

Children from South Africa, Ecuador, Canada and China, after addressing the Johannesburg Earth Summit in September 2002.

Zimbabwe

Some or all of these peace deals may, of course, fall through. In the meantime, other conflicts continue. Liberia often seems on the verge of slipping back into chaos and Somalia remains at the mercy of its warring **clans**. In the south, the stability and prospects of Zimbabwe – and, to some extent, Namibia – have been undermined by the incompetence and corruption of their respective governments.

Robert Mugabe has ruled Zimbabwe since 1980, when his ZANU-PF party won the elections that marked the end of **white minority government**. Mugabe initially proclaimed his commitment to a **democratic**, multiracial Zimbabwe, and the white farmers who provided the country with most of its export earnings were encouraged to stay. However, over the next decade Mugabe created a one-party-state and awarded himself increasingly **dictatorial** powers. White-owned farms that fell vacant for one reason or another were generally given to his political allies, rather than divided up between black Zimbabweans in desperate need of land. Mugabe's resemblance to Mobutu grew more pronounced, and Zimbabwe gained a reputation as the latest African kleptocracy.

Zimbabwe's President Robert Mugabe greets supporters during an election rally in June 2000.

The 1990s were hard on African economies, and in Zimbabwe corruption and inefficient management made matters worse. As political dissatisfaction rose among the poor black majority, Mugabe tried deflecting the blame on to the country's white farmers and their supporters in the outside world. His followers were encouraged to invade and take over the farms, and several of the farmers were murdered. As lawlessness spread, the economy declined still further, and in 2002 famine seemed a real possibility.

Mugabe ignored the rulings of his own judges, and fixed elections in his own favour. By 2002 he had gone a long way towards destroying the country's political and economic inheritances, for no better reason than keeping himself in power. In the meantime, he and his generals were making the most of the war in the Congo, taking a profitable slice of that country's diamond trade in exchange for protecting the Kabila government.

His example spread to Namibia, where Sam Nujoma's SWAPO also came to power after a long **guerrilla** war against white minority rule. Here too, the government seemed more interested in **scapegoating** white farmers than in taking the necessary legal steps towards a fairer distribution of the available land. A growing lawlessness was allowed to threaten a tourist industry which provided a sizable portion of the country's income. Namibia's intervention in the Congo, like Zimbabwe's, was mostly an expedition in search of loot.

Mozambique

In recent years, a much more positive example of African development has been provided by Zimbabwe's eastern neighbour Mozambique. Like Angola, Mozambique was given independence by the Portuguese in 1975. Its Soviet-supported government fought a long and destructive guerrilla war against South African-supported Renamo rebels, which was only brought to a peaceful conclusion when both the Soviet Union and white South Africa collapsed. Unlike Jonas Savimbi in Angola, the Renamo leader Alfonso Dhlakama accepted his defeat in elections, and the healing process was allowed to begin. Since then, Mozambique has enjoyed one of the fastest growing economies in Africa. It has diversified its agriculture, growing cotton, sugar and cashew nuts for export, and a variety of other crops for feeding its own population. Small and medium-sized industries have been successfully launched.

Mozambique has great potential. Firstly, it has peace, which makes everything else possible. Secondly, it has abundant supplies of energy – coal, gas and hydro-electric power from the huge Cabora Dam left behind by the Portuguese – which saves the country an enormous amount of money. Thirdly, it has a good government in which corruption is not out of control. Because of these three advantages, the government has been able to provide what international financial institutions like the IMF want – a Mozambique attractive to Western business – without further impoverishing its own

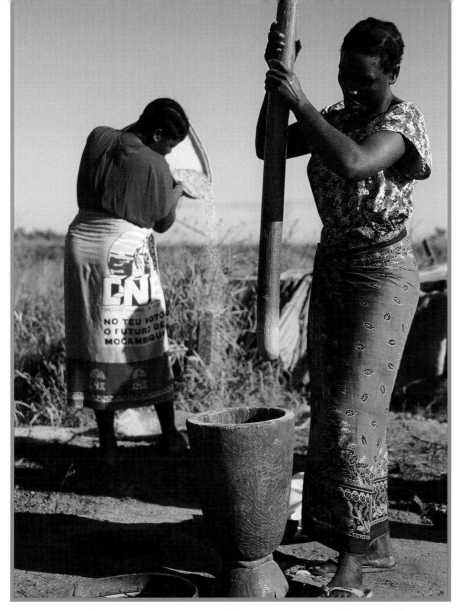

Two Mozambican women at work in a cooperatively-owned rice field during the 1990s.

people. And this in turn has given rise to a fourth advantage – the West has rewarded Mozambique by giving the country above-average **debt relief**.

Mozambique remains very poor: life expectancy is only 35 years and 70 per cent of its population still live below the **poverty line**. The government must now ensure that all its citizens share in the country's new Western-generated prosperity. If it succeeds in this – a task which has proved beyond most African governments – then the future will be bright.

Prospects

Africa's problems are enormous. Who is more to blame for this – the Africans themselves or the Western powers that control the world economy? Clearly, neither are blameless. **Colonialism** deepened divisions within African societies and froze African economies in a subservient position. In the 40 years since independence, **Cold War** attitudes and Western business interests have ensured that nothing fundamental has changed. But Africans too must take some responsibility for the continent's plight. The ruling elites of post-independence Africa have all too often proved **corrupt**, incompetent and brutal.

Sub-Saharan Africa is caught in a vicious circle. Economic failure and poverty lead to dislocation and violence, which deter Western companies from investing in Africa's future. Without such investment, failures multiply and poverty deepens. During the 1990s there was an enormous surge of growth in the world economy, but Africa missed out on this growth. There were too many wars, too much havoc, too many safer places for the world's leading corporations and financial institutions to place their investments.

What can be done?
In September 2002 British Prime Minister Tony Blair called the continent's problems 'a scar on the conscience of our world'. The rest of the world, he said, had 'a duty to heal it'. Blair's government, however, has made no attempt to rein in the big multinational corporations, whose unwavering pursuit of profits keeps Africa poor. African coffee growers, for example, receive well under 10 per cent of the money Western supermarkets charge for a jar of instant coffee, barely enough to cover their costs. The profits are in processing, distribution and sales, all of which are controlled by the corporations. They have no interest in paying the growers more than they have to.

Only Western consumers have the power to force a change in corporate behaviour, and over the last decade increasing numbers have chosen to buy non-corporate 'Fair Trade' products, which provide the growers with much fairer rewards for their labours. Western charities provide emergency support in times of acute crisis and help to supply the knowledge and technology that Africans need to help themselves. Many Western individuals, working through organizations like the American Peace Corps, the British VSO (Voluntary Service Overseas) or the French-based

Médicins Sans Frontières (Doctors Without Borders), give their time, effort and skill to help a continent so much poorer than their own. They work alongside many Africans who are also determined to improve conditions.

Workers on a plantation in Ghana. These organic bananas are sold under the Fair Trade label.

Such aid is enormously valuable, but it can never be enough. In 19th-century Britain, where the poorer section of the population suffered while the rich thrived, people eventually realized that the free market, left to itself, was unable to solve the problem, and would in fact make matters worse. The free market had to be put on hold, while those unable to help themselves were given a helping hand. In today's world, Africa needs much the same helping hand, but the prospects are not good. Those who thrived in 19th-century Britain needed the labour of those who suffered, and eventually needed their votes to remain in power.

Africa has many resources the world needs and wants, but no world government to which it can appeal for necessary help. There are, however, reasons to hope. In West Africa, Senegal is peaceful, stable and relatively prosperous, whilst Nigeria, despite having significant troubles, has recently elected a democratic government. Botswana continues to strengthen its democratic system. And whilst AIDS is a potentially disastrous problem, Uganda has managed to create a programme that has reduced the rate of infection in that country.

Appendix
Chronology of events

1480 Portuguese explore West African coast

1900 Virtually all of Africa colonized

1957-64 Most sub-Saharan countries receive independence

1961 Eritrea's struggle for independence from Ethiopia begins

1963 Organization of African Unity (OAU) founded

Civil war breaks out in Sudan

1964 Tanganyika and Zanzibar unite to form Tanzania

1965 Mobutu takes over in the Democratic Republic of the Congo

1967-70 Civil war in Nigeria

1971 Amin seizes power in Uganda

1972 End of the first Sudanese civil war

1973-4 Huge oil price rises follow Arab-Israeli War of October 1973

1974 Revolution in Ethiopia

1975 Portugal gives independence to Angola and Mozambique. Civil wars begin in both countries.

1977 Somalia invades Ethiopia's Ogaden region

1978 Amin invades Tanzania

1979 Amin overthrown in Uganda after invading Tanzania

Bokassa overthrown in Central African Republic

1980 Doe seizes power in Liberia

1981 Rawlings seizes power for the second time in Ghana

1983 Second civil war begins in Sudan

1984 Famine in Ethiopia

1989 Civil war begins in Liberia

1990 Central authority collapses in Somalia

Cold War ends. Soviets begin withdrawal from Ethiopia and Angola.

1991 Dergue overthrown in Ethiopia

Agreements to end the civil wars in Angola and Mozambique

Civil wars begin in Sierra Leone

1992 Government wins elections in Angola

1993 UNITA restarts civil war in Angola

Eritrea achieves independence from Ethiopia

1994 Genocide in Rwanda

1995-6 Genocidaires find refuge in the Congo (then Zaire)

1996 Rwanda invades the Congo in alliance with Laurent Kabila

1997 Congolese leader Mobutu replaced by Kabila

Elections in Liberia

1998 Rwanda invades the Congo for the second time

Obasanjo wins presidential election in Nigeria

1998-2000 War between Ethiopia and Eritrea

1998-2002 Growing Muslim-Christian violence in Nigeria

2002 Peace deals to end civil wars in Sierra Leone, Angola, Sudan and the Congo

Johannesburg summit on Sustainable Development

Further reading

Africa in Crisis (educational pack) (Save The Children, 1993)

Brogan, Patrick, *World Conflicts* (Bloomsbury, 1998)

Fage, J. D. with Tordoff, William, *A History of Africa* (Routledge, 2002)

Freeman, Charles, *Crisis in Central Africa* (Wayland, 1998)

Ricciuti, Edward R., *Somalia, A Crisis of Famine and War* (Evans, 1995)

Schwab, Peter, *Africa: A Continent Self-Destructs* (Palgrave, 2001)

Shillington, Dr Kevin, *Independence in Africa* (Evans, 1997).

Useful websites

www.amnesty.org
Amnesty International

http://www.cnn.com/World
CNN

http://news.bbc.co.uk/1/low/world/africa
BBC African news

Glossary

Arab member of ethnic group that originated in Arabia, but which now inhabits much of North Africa and the Middle East

ceasefire an agreed end to a period of fighting

cholera life-threatening bacterial infection usually caused by sewage-contaminated food or water

Christianity one of the world's three major monotheistic (one God) religions (along with Judaism and Islam)

civil war war between different groups in one country

clans social groups based on membership of large, extended families

Cold War period of political hostility from 1945-90 between the USA and its allies and the Soviet Union and its communist allies

colonial preference rules of trade that forced colonies to buy and sell from the European countries that administered them

colony country or area that is ruled by another country

communism political theory and practice that puts the interests of society as a whole above the interests of individuals

constitution in politics, the way a country is set up to safeguard its fundamental principles

corrupt involved in corruption

corruption immoral practices like bribery, fraud and other forms of financial theft

coup violent seizure of power

debt relief being let off either all or part of a debt

democracy political system in which governments are regularly elected by the people, or a country in which this system exists

dictatorial behaving like a dictator: not taking any notice of anyone else's views or interests

dictatorship unrestricted rule by a single person or small group

ethnic relating to different cultural or racial groups

free enterprise economic and political system in which individuals rather than governments make most of the decisions about which goods and services are produced, and how they are bought and sold

general strike refusal of workers in all industries to work

genocidaires those responsible for genocide, particularly that in Rwanda

genocide murder or attempted murder of an entire ethnic group

global warming the gradual warming of the Earth's atmosphere, mostly caused by rising levels of carbon dioxide

guerrilla unofficial soldier

human rights rights which should belong to any person

idealistic having the hope and belief that things can be dramatically improved

infrastructure material, technological and economic foundations of a society

Islam one of world's three major monotheistic (one God)

religions (along with Christianity and Judaism), founded by the Prophet Muhammad in the 7th century

literacy ability to read and write

military dictatorship government by unelected members of the armed forces

Muslim follower of Islam

Organization of African Unity (OAU) association of African states formed in 1963 for mutual cooperation

persecute treat someone with continual cruelty and unfairness

poverty line level of income, varying from country to country, below which somebody is considered to be living in poverty

refugee one who flees for safety, usually to another country

safety zone area in which protection is provided for civilians during a conflict, usually by neutral or foreign troops

scapegoat person or group blamed for other people's failures

shanty town large area of roughly-built shelters adjoining a town where the poorest people live

Sharia law collection of laws derived from verses in the Muslim holy book, the Qur'an

socialism a set of ideas that puts more stress on the needs of the community as a whole and less on the short-term wants or needs of the individual

stereotype typical example, often exaggerated or inaccurate

sub-Saharan Africa Africa south of the Sahara Desert

superpower powerful country with more economic, political and military power than most; usually refers to the USA and the Soviet Union

trade union organization set up by working people to protect and improve their pay and conditions

tribe social grouping of varying size, which may be based on one or more of several factors such as: language, related clans, ethnic identification, or a shared geographical region

United Nations (UN) international body set up in 1945 to promote peace and cooperation between states

white minority government government by the descendants of white European immigrants in countries where the majority of the poulation were black Africans. Such governments existed in South Africa (until 1993), Rhodesia (until 1979 when it became Zimbabwe) and South West Africa (until 1990 when it became Namibia).

world recession a general slowdown of global economic activity (as occurred in the years following the 1973 rise in oil prices)

Index

Titles in the *Troubled World* series include:

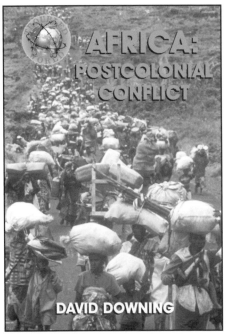

Hardback   0 431 18364 3

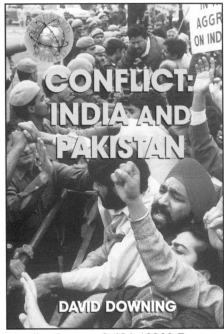

Hardback   0 431 18362 7

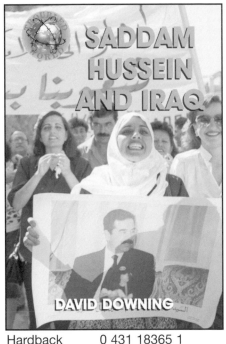

Hardback   0 431 18365 1

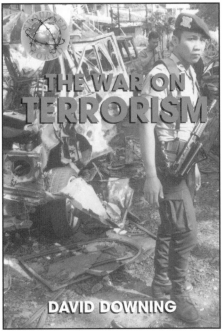

Hardback   0 431 18363 5

Find out about the other titles in this series on our website www.heinemann.co.uk/library